Communication for Couples

13 Ways to Better Communication in Your Relationship

Maria Hall

Table of Contents

The information in the following pages is broadly considered to be a truthful and accurate account of facts, and as such any inattention, use or misuse of the information in question by the reader will render any resulting actions solely under their purview. There are no scenarios in which the publisher or the original author of this work can be in any fashion deemed liable for any hardship or damages that may befall them after undertaking information described herein.

Additionally, the information found on the following pages is intended for informational purposes only and should thus be considered, universal. As befitting its nature, the information presented is without assurance regarding its continued validity or interim quality. Trademarks that mentioned are done without written consent and can in no way be considered an endorsement from the trademark holder.

Introduction

I want to thank you for purchasing *Communication for Couples*.

It is no secret that effective communication in today's world is at an all-time low. Ironically, you would think that with all the new advancements in technology, communicating with those important to us would be a breeze, right? In reality, smartphones and other devices have actually managed to place a rift between us and the positive development of our core relationships.

Communication between couples, no matter how long people have been together, is an essential piece to making things work long-term, through the good, the bad, and the ugly that life inevitably throws our way.

Within the chapters of this book, you will discover and perhaps relate to why our society blatantly sucks at communication, a variety of tips and techniques to better understand communication and the importance it holds within your own relationship, how to hone your nonverbal and sexual communication, and much more.

I have struggled with my share of relationships in the past, typically due to the other person's lack of being able to communicate their thoughts and feelings. It wasn't until I started to dig deeper into the psychology of it all that I realized how vital being able to positively and effectively communicate aided in the strength of a partnership with another human being.

Yes, there are tons of books out there on bettering your communication skills, but I challenge you to read this book in its entirety so that you can discover your problem areas and fix them before it is too late. Thanks again for purchasing my book. Every effort was made to ensure it is full of as much useful information as possible, please enjoy!

Chapter 1: Why Our Society Struggles in Communication

Communication is the action we all take as creatures of the planet to inform others how we feel, what we think, and much more. In the past three decades, technology has drastically revolutionized how we talk to one another as a race. Technology can link us to others in real time all around the world. It's pretty awesome, right?

Certainly, but what many of us fail to realize is how these advancements have changed the world of communication. While there are many positives to being connected almost constantly, there *are* negative effects that we have started to see over the last few years.

Universal Distraction

Mobile devices of all shapes, sizes, and brands allow us to remain connected to others, even when we are away from our bulky computers. This is great, especially if emergencies were to arise, but it is also a distraction that many are still oblivious to. Cellular devices are not just dangerously distracting while behind the wheel, but they also keep us from being productive at work and school. Having messaging applications present at all time draws the attention away from users and their priorities, one of those being able to effectively communicate in their relationships.

We are Becoming Dehumanized

Technology is *powerful* in both positive and negative ways. The internet has allowed us to surf and speak to others anonymously and allowed us to explore and communicate with others with no need for personal details. However, this can lead to people acting differently when they finally meet up with those they have been talking to over the internet face-to-face.

The internet has made talking a faceless activity, which is molding society to be extremely terrible at in-human communication. This is especially true of the younger generations, who have been born and grown up with these avenues of technology all their lives. Thanks to the internet, we are inhibiting ourselves to learn the basics of conversing with other people, which is essentially making us lack personality.

Isolation Socially

With the creation of elaborate social networks online, there is almost no need to go out into the real world and talk to others in person. This is causing a drastic rise in social isolation. Just like any skill, if you never practice it, you will lose it. The same goes for your communication skills. There is a major difference between being able to talk to someone with the assistance of a device versus in person.

Changes the Effectiveness of Creating Bonds with Others

When you are constantly checking your phone every five minutes and scrolling endlessly and mindlessly through your social media newsfeed, you are taking attention away from creating a real connection with those in your life that you meet. This could be a red flag at the start of relationships.

Thanks to texting, the times are long gone when we patiently await a phone call from the person we went on dates with. Talking to anyone is at your disposal 24/7. When you never truly miss anyone, this can hurt the bond you have with others as well.

Overall, it is no secret whatsoever that we as a race have become awful at basic communication. There are a large number of relationships, from budding to getting engaged to getting married that end tragically just because the parties involved in the relationship failed to learn to communicate properly.

Thankfully, if you and your loved one are having issues conversing and truly communicating with one another, there are tons of things you can start to implement *today* that can help you get on the same page and back into a 'happily ever after' story.

Chapter 2: Avoid the Communication Pitfalls

For effective communication in *any* relationship, there are several drawbacks that you should *always* navigate around. The following pitfalls are ones that many of us have encountered before but having the right skills to properly respond to them is *essential*. Especially for couples.

To Communicate, The First Thing To Do Is Talk!

If you are angry, upset, or just generally bothered by something, you aren't doing either of you *any* favors by trying to spare feelings or avoid an argument. If you bottle it in then there's a good chance you're going to 'blow' somewhere down the road and end up hurting them anyway. Or having an even bigger fight that heads down roads neither of you really wants to go.

How can they fix it if they don't know it's 'broken'? The only way to properly deal with anything troubling you in the relationship is to start a conversation about it.

Never Go On The Attack!

If you make the issue personal for your partner by saying things like "I *hate* that you do this all the time" or, even worse, "I can't believe you were so *stupid*" there's more than a decent chance that they are immediately going to turn defensive and may even attack back. When either or both of you are on the attack then at least one of you isn't listening; that is when it is impossible to effectively communicate.

Pause! If you are steamed about something, then don't speak immediately. Stop and think about what you want to say and try to flip it around so that you talk about you and not about your partner. Try using starters such as, "It really hurts me when you XYZ" or "I think" or "I feel." If you start the conversation with explaining nicely how the issue affected or affects you, then your partner is less likely to feel that it's necessary to stop listening and defend themselves. This helps keep the conversation on target without devolving into an argument over whether what you said is correct or not. How can they dispute what you said when it was about yourself?

Less Is More

Don't drone on about it! After you have stated your initial starter, it is always a good idea to stop and listen. Give them a chance to reply and address your point or ask a question without you having added flair, embellishments, or additional items that can actually conceal the main message or completely disrupt the whole intended line of conversation. When we try to over-explain or simplify the issue by continuing to add to the message, you will likely end up in a totally unintended conversation.

Stop Repeating Yourself! Stop Repeating Yourself!

Again this goes back to the Pause feature. Don't keep saying the same thing over and over or rephrasing it in an attempt to get your message across. Stop and let them respond. Then if you need to clarify you can rephrase without taking the chance of them 'tuning you out' and if they don't appear to be responding with the appropriate level of importance to the subject you can say something such as, "It is really important that we talk about this. How do *you* think we should handle it?"

Putting the spotlight on them and their feelings will lessen the chances of defensiveness or personal attacks. It also helps ensure that they do indeed understand the gravity of the issue and that you get your message across in a concise manner as possible.

No Take Backs!

Once more we return you to our regularly scheduled Pause. Stopping to think before you start the discussion will help avoid you saying something you immediately regret or want to qualify. If you have to backpedal to try and neutralize what was said then the entire reason for the dialog can be lost in the fluff. If you immediately have to add something like, "Not to hurt your feelings" or "What I mean to say is..." then you run the chance of counteracting your intended message.

Think about what you want to say and start the conversation with confidence that you can stand behind what you say.

You Wouldn't Like Me When I'm Angry

Okay, this is one trap that many stumble into and it's easily avoidable. Don't ever start the conversation with, "Can I say something without you getting mad" or "Not to hurt your feelings, but." Starting like this will immediately make them defensive as they will expect an attack and chances are they are indeed going to end up hurt or mad and not hear your message at all. Don't put a handicap on your message before you even have a chance to voice it, there's no need to justify what you need to say. Hit that Pause and think about what you want to say.

Stay Off The Phone!

Going back to what I said earlier about the digital age, it is never a good idea to start a serious conversation via text. Words can be taken wrong and totally skew or destroy the intended message. The level of importance is almost impossible to convey digitally and behind a phone or computer, there is always the chance you may unintentionally say something hurtful. If it's important to you then it can wait until you're in person.

Don't Come In Unprepared

The best way to handle difficult conversations is preparation. Have an idea of what you think is needed to fix the issue and deliver your message with actionable feedback. You can't just present an issue and expect them to completely fix everything on their own. Define the issue, address any specific undesirable or detrimental behaviors, explain the impact of their actions/inactions, and give at least one idea on how you think it's best to address the specific issue.

Follow Through

If, for whatever reason, now isn't a good time to have the conversation, explain why you cannot speak right now, set a time to discuss it, and then *make sure* that you keep that appointment. The same goes for any agreements or promises that arise throughout the discussion. You can't just say it. You have to do it.

Many times we are tempted to tell them what they want or need to hear at the time, only to devalue their concerns by not really addressing the issue at hand. Failing to follow through can lead to distrust and, of course, hurt feelings and even resentment.

Chapter 3: How Better Communication Leads to a Healthier Relationship

Listening is vital in creating proper dialogue, which in turn is essential to maintaining a healthy relationship. When there's a communication breakdown there's always a chance for misunderstandings and confusion that can lead to bitterness, or the development of overall poor communication between you.

Without open lines of communication with our partner, they can feel unsupported, unappreciated, and even unwanted. Relationships that want to last are built on honesty, openness, trust, and mutual respect. Building a productive, supportive, and caring relationship is only possible if we develop effective communication skills.

Communication is a two-way street and include compromise. We have to be able to honestly voice our feelings because keeping things bottled-up can foster malcontent and can even be detrimental to our overall health. When we focus on listening to our significant other, and they listen to us, it is less likely that there will be misunderstandings.

We all tend to 'vent' sometimes and of course, there are times when that is indeed necessary and even therapeutic. But if there is an issue that seriously needs to be addressed and resolved and we simply go on a mad rant instead of discussing it calmly, chances are high that our partner will just think we are just blowing off steam and may well just tune us out. Get those rants out when necessary but remember the items we've discussed so far and strive to convey your grievance clearly. Without it sounding like it's something you just need to 'get off your chest.'

When we feel that we have really been listened to, and not just 'heard,' it helps us validate that our partner does value our opinion and feelings. Thinking that we're underappreciated or not respected doesn't work at school or at our jobs and it certainly won't work in a relationship – not one that has any hope of lasting long-term.

When we are properly communicating, then our focus is on each other and nothing else. This always helps bring us closer together and helps ensure a healthy relationship.

Chapter 4: Basic Communication Skills ALL Couples Need to Develop

While we've already discussed a few of the basic skills necessary for effective communication, there are a few essential abilities that we must harness and develop to maintain a healthy relationship. So, we'll go a little deeper into them here and try to break them down.

Listening

Hearing and listening are two completely different things. When we only hear someone we can miss emphasis, words, and even whole ideas. But when we actively pay attention to the speaker and use the listen very eagerly, we become more effective listeners. Following the skills below can help you improve your listening skills:

Clear your mind and avoid mental wandering. Don't get distracted by trying to decide what you want to say next or even focusing on other things on your mind.

Focus on what they are saying. Give them your full attention and listen carefully to what they are saying.

Never interrupt them. Always allow them to talk without interruption until they get to the point that they need to make.

Maintain good eye contact. If you aren't looking at them then they are likely to think you aren't listening.

Avoid clenching your fists, rolling your eyes, or shaking your head. These reactions can lead us to focus on what *was* said, and not what is being said now. Body language can easily encourage or discourage the other person to speak.

Stay away from distractions. Don't pick at your fingernails, go digging through your purse, or start paying attention to the television. These items can distract the speaker and make it really difficult for you to actively listen.

Acknowledge what they say. Show that you are interested in what they are saying and encourage them to continue speaking with acknowledging responses such as "of course," "I understand," "okay," and even "uh-huh.' Sitting in complete silence can make them feel as if we are not truly hearing them.

When it's your turn to speak, paraphrase what they just said. This helps confirm that you have been listening, and ensure that you understand correctly before addressing what was said. And just to make sure you are both on the same page, you may want to summarize the discussion at the end of the conversation.

Pay attention to their tone and body language. This can clue you in on how they are responding to what you say and even hint at what they are thinking and feeling.

Let them know that you value what they are saying by responding constructively, even if you disagree. Stay away from ridiculing, criticizing, dismissing, or diverting the conversation.

After making sure that you completely understand what they are saying, **respond appropriately.** Never overreact and try not to take it personal. Address the underlying issue and not the person themselves.

Discussing Sensitive or Touchy Subjects

When dealing with difficult issues effective communication skills are essential. While these skills are always important, they become critical when we have to discuss things that neither of you really wants to.

Don't put off what needs to be discussed today. Dealing with issues today rather than tomorrow, helps us maintain objectivity, avoid misinformation, keep our self-control, and hopefully prevent it from escalating.

While it can be uncomfortable, **you may have to be the conversation starter.** Try using a question rather than a statement, such as "I really need your help. Can we talk about something?"

Set up a time to talk privately where you won't be distracted, disrupted, or overheard.

Practice what you want to say ahead of time. Be specific about the issue and if you are uncomfortable discussing the issue, you may even want to role-play the conversation with a trusted friend.

Allow them to voice their opinion and point of view to reduce feelings of defensiveness. This also encourages them to be open and more receptive to what you have to say.

It is usually best to **keep explanations short & simple.** Tailor the message to the person you're speaking with while keeping in mind any possible sensitivities.

Be honest! Always address all of the issues in a straightforward and honest manner. Trust is built on honesty. Don't try to sugarcoat but also don't be mean. Give them your honest opinion on the matter.

Allow them to converse at a pace that's comfortable for them. Remember that they may need to formulate their thoughts and replies or may even need some time to completely absorb and reflect on what you've said. Don't get impatient. Even if you have to put the entire conversation on pause and discuss it later when they have had time to digest the dialogue.

Remember, while this may be a difficult topic for you it can also be quite upsetting for the other person to hear. While you cannot control their reactions, you can indeed anticipate them. Be prepared and emotionally ready for a negative response from them.

If the conversation devolves into hostility, hit that pause button. Set and agree a time to resume the discussion and then, of course, follow through.

Communicate Assertively

Speaking up for yourself while respecting the rights of your significant other to do the same demonstrates that you are willing to stand up for yourself, your rights, and interests. Assertive communication is built on mutual respect and also shows that you are empathetic and willing to work together to reach a mutually satisfying result.

This allows you to act in your own best interests, including actually refusing a request, and demonstrates your self-respect, your expectations for respect, and your willingness to give respect.

Convey a clear, concise, and confident message. Be specific, positive, and use "I" statements.

It's okay to say no but if you do so, give an explanation why but do not apologize or make excuses for saying no.

Use a clear and firm but pleasant tone of voice.

Lay out the issue and the desired outcome.

Stay on target. Never digress or allow yourself to be derailed into other issues, and paraphrase or restate to reassure them that you are listening to them as well.

Always validate the other person's feelings on the issues. Acknowledge how they feel and address what needs to be taken care of.

Speaking

The overall goal of the conversation is to ensure that your partner understands exactly what your message is. Therefore, it is vital that we hone our communication and speaking skills.

Have your objective ready, be organized, and structure the conversation toward reaching that goal. Take the time to think before you speak and present it in a thought out and structured manner.

Maintain eye contact and use their name throughout the conversation to ensure that you have the other person's attention.

Always present your issue in a way that is appropriate for the problem at hand and emotional state of the other person. You may also want to consider the age and sex of who you are speaking with.

Use open-ended questions that elicit a response instead of just yes or no replies, such as "what do you think about..." or "tell me about..."

Honestly share your feelings, but be respectful. Try to think of it as an opportunity for them to learn something about you.

Avoid those generalizing statements like "never," or "always."

Focus on your feelings and use phrases such as, "I feel," or "I need."

Be generous and specific with praise. We have to make sure that positive feedback outshines the negative or any criticism. Focus on their positive points and try to maintain a positive perspective throughout.

Be calm, positive, and respectful. Respond, but do not react. If you feel that they are taking it personally or the conversation has diverted down a dead end alley, then it's probably time to hit that pause button.

Try to resolve the conflict, not win an argument. Remember that sometimes you may have to agree to disagree but you should always attempt to develop a solution to the overall issue.

Don't get hung up on the tiny details. Maintain focus and give the main points of what you need to discuss.

Chapter 5: Tips to Communicate More Effectively

There are a couple of rules that you should always remember to effectively communicate with your partner.

1 - Give yourself time to calm down. If they have done something that truly upsets or angers you, of course, you need to discuss it. But that doesn't mean it has to be done right away. Give yourself 48 hours and if you're still upset, then start the conversation with the knowledge that you have given yourself time to reflect on the issue. If it is no longer bothering you then you may want to consider just dropping it altogether.

2 - Pick the right time to have the conversation. Pick a time when you can both discuss the issue calmly without distractions, stress, or being in a rush. You may even want to schedule a time to overcome any possible hurdles.

3 - Stay away from beast mode. Choose your words carefully without cursing or name-calling so that you do not come across as harsh or uncaring. Never go on the attack. That makes it personal and of course, they will automatically go on the defensive.

4 - Dig to find the real issue. Many times our partner may be upset or angry over one thing, but end up starting an argument over something completely different. Use

probing and open-ended questions to get to the root of the matter.

5 - Compromise! While it may be easy to say, it is sometimes hard to do. Try to find a middle ground that allows both of you to feel satisfied with the outcome.

6 - Always keep their feelings in mind. If you are in a relationship then it stands to reason that you care about your partner and their feelings. Don't say something that invalidates their feelings for what they are saying.

Chapter 6: Expert Tips to Communicate Better in Your Relationship

Better communication is a skill that almost every relationship could handle some enhancement on. Even when the subject matter is not important, or maybe even mundane, we should always attempt to fully communicate within our relationship.

Talk more! Don't just wait until something is bothering you to have a conversation with your significant other. Talk to them about your day, the book you're reading, or what you have planned for tomorrow. Far too often these days, couples park in front of the computer or television and barely speak throughout an entire evening. If we only have discussions about things that are wrong, then our loved one may well come to expect this and shut us out before we even get to state what the real issue is. At least once a week shut down those electronics and spend time just talking about yourselves.

Never lie! Little lies turn into big lies and can end up causing many more problems than you began with. Be honest.

Don't use the silent treatment. This is a huge barrier to good communication. Trying to punish them by not speaking to them is only putting off the issue and can lead to flared tempers and resentment.

Be open! This may mean talking about things you have never discussed with anyone else but means you are being unabashedly honest and vulnerable with them. While this may open yourself up to possible disappointment or being hurt, it can also lead to opening yourself up to your partner and the full potential of all a relationship can be.

Watch for any nonverbal signals. Their body language, eye contact, tone of voice and its inflection are all aspects of nonverbal communication. If they have their arms folded in front of them it may mean they are currently defensive or feeling closed off and a lack of eye contact can mean that they are not listening, not interested, or find the conversation difficult to talk about. A more aggressive or louder tone may mean their emotions are getting the better of them and they are escalating the discussion and may also hint that they feel like they have not been understood or heard.

Stay on target. Don't get distracted by escalating the conversation to who does what around the house, who takes care of the children more, or whose fault it actually is. While it may seem easy to throw in a cheap shot or try to cram in everything you think the conversation seems to call for, you may never reach a mutually satisfying resolution if the discussion devolves into an argument or evolves into 14 conversations about things that really have no bearing on the subject at hand.

Never assume that either of you is a mind reader. Many people make the mistake of thinking that their partner knows their thoughts and position on just about everything. If you assume that you already know how they feel, you generally tanned to react to that assumption rather than how they really feel. So, while you should never assume you know how they will react, you should also never assume that they do or should already completely understand your thoughts and feelings on the matter.

Read between the lines. While you are working on communicating better, try to remember that your partner may not quite be up to your skill level. Is what they are saying the actual true issue? If you need to, use those probing and open-ended questions to help you decipher the coded message.

Chapter 7: Experience the Miracle of Communication with these Easy Tools

There are several quick and easy tools at your disposal to help you effectively communicate better in your relationship. Some of them may seem a little strange at first, but with a little fine-tuning and tweaking to suit you, your partner, and your needs can help foster better communication skills all around.

Clear eyes – If you don't fully understand what is being said or asked of you, ask them to clarify. This is especially important when the topic is emotional or is clearly upsetting your partner. The lack of clear communication will just leave you both frustrated and disappointed.

Technology! While the technology of cell phones and computers can be detrimental to her relationship if overused or abused, they can also be a great tool to start the building blocks of great communication. Send your special someone something just to make them laugh and brighten their day, or utilize the technology to increase your intimacy in connection with some good old-fashioned flirting. Being able to make them laugh or even blush helps increase the desire on both sides to have even more nonverbal type communications.

Remember to H.A.L.T. - If you are Hungry, Angry, Loopy, or Tired then it's not a good time to have a conversation. Get yourself something to eat, give yourself time to calm down, take a good hot shower or bath, or relax and get some rest before attempting to start that conversation.

That pause button - If things end up getting to be heated or headed into galaxies better left unexplored, then the best practice is to put the conversation on ice and come back to it later. Agree to let it lie for now and go grab something to eat together, watch a movie, or even spend some time alone. Many times you will find that issues that seem so important now, just don't seem so world-breaking the following day.

Trust is a key ingredient - If you lie, even about little things or to spare your partner's feelings, and they find out the truth, it can and will damage the relationship. Being honest and trustworthy can save you both a lot of pain down the road.

Appropriate & neutral ground - Don't try to start a conversation while they are cooking dinner or watching their favorite team on TV. Likewise, you don't want to discuss money issues while in bed nor do you want to discuss any private issues in the front yard or while visiting friends. Pick an appropriate time and place to begin the conversation.

Remember 'Go, Dog, Go?' Well now it's time to learn "What, How, What?" You need to explain exactly *What* the issue is, *How* it affects you or makes you feel, and *What* you think should be done to resolve it. Using this as an outline before starting the conversation can help ensure that the pertinent points are covered.

There is no "'you" in communication - Remember I, I, I. I feel, I need, I want. Keep it about yourself and stay off the attack by not turning the issue personal for them.

Chapter 8: Therapy Exercises to Improve Communication

There are several therapy exercises for couples that center on practicing skills to help make you and your partner better listeners and reduce conflict while creating a more efficient and effective way for you to share how you feel. Utilizing these tools can help you to better express yourself and lead to a healthier and fulfilling relationship. Learning to turn communication into a strength as opposed to a liability will help ensure a much happier relationship and help you and your partner grow even closer as you gain a new level of appreciation and understanding of one another.

Active listening requires that you fully concentrate, respond, understand, and retain what has been said. Active listening is designed to help make it easier to discuss sensitive issues and to deepen your appreciation, empathy, and understanding of your partner.

Reflective listening is where you paraphrase what they have said back to them to confirm that both of you completely understand.

One of the single most effective ways to create a better and more efficient communication style is by only using positive language. Make a strong and concerted effort to adopt an encouraging tone along with non-abusive and non-accusatory words and phrases. Stay away from name-calling, swearing, and the ever unpopular "you always" and "you never."

Another great exercise is known as 'the miracle question.' This can help you to learn about your partner's desires and dreams as well as explore your own and gain an understanding what you both need to be happy in the relationship. Simply ask your spouse 'while you are asleep tonight, a miracle occurs. When you wake up in the morning, what changes would tell you that our life had suddenly gotten better?' While their answer may be a complete impossibility, it can still give you a lot of insight and be very useful.

Soul gazing is an intense exercise that can help couples connect on a much deeper level. The exercise is simple but can have a huge impact on the couple's sense of connectedness. Simply face your partner in a seated position and move close to one another so that your knees are almost touching. Look into each other's eyes and hold eye contact for 3 to 5 minutes while refraining from talking. If the silence is uncomfortable to you, put on some music that you both like and hold eye contact until the song is through. This exercise may be uncomfortable or awkward at first, but if you practice it a few times a week it will help deepen the connection between the partners and help strengthen the lines of communication.

A simple yet powerful exercise is called Uninterrupted Listening. This exercise is exactly what it sounds like. You simply set a timer for 3 to 5 minutes and let your partner speak. They can talk about whatever they wish and your job is to do one thing and one thing only: listen. You are not to speak until the timer goes off, completely getting your partner your undivided attention. While you may not speak while the timer is going, you are allowed to use your nonverbal communication skills to encourage your partner or to show empathy. Once the timer is up, switch places, reset the timer and complete the exercise again with you having the floor. This exercise can help the two of you strengthen the lines of communication by getting you to talk to each other just about your day or what is on your mind. This is a great exercise to use on a regular basis and you'll find that the more you use it, the more comfortable you both are sharing your day with each other.

Another easy exercise is called '5 Things,' and can be utilized anytime the two of you are together. You only need your imagination. You just come up with the theme, such as; "what I appreciate in you," "what I'm grateful for," or "what I would like us to do together." And then you each take a turn listing off five things within the chosen theme. Once you've finished sharing both of your lists, take the time to ask follow-up questions, comment on each other's answers, or come up with five more things together. This can be a very fun and engaging exercise that can help couples to connect and learn something new about their partner.

Mix it up a little. When we follow the same routine day in and day out it can cause the relationship to grow stale or even stagnant. Leave the distractions at home and share some time together in a new environment so that you can both relax and unwind. Taking a trip together it is a great opportunity for you to work on building those good communication skills while having a little fun together in a whole new place and creating new memories. This can also help alleviate any stress that could possibly be making communication more difficult for you. There are also some great couple's retreats where the sole purpose is to help you improve your relationship.

Learn to grow *with* your partner, not against or away from them. Of course, we all tend to grow, change, and expand our horizons over time but when you are in a long-term relationship can sometimes make it easy for us to be blinded to changes in our partner's likes, dislikes, interests, or even new aspects of their personality. Keeping the lines of communication open and attempting to share their interests or hobbies can help you stay in tune with any changes.

One last exercise that I want to share with you is a great little communication activity that is great for those needing to make changes or to solve difficult relationship issues. This exercise keeps the discussion light but can remind you of the special connection you have with your partner and help you learn more about them and yourself. As always, be mindful of your nonverbal communication and simply take turns asking each other a question from the topics listed below. You can make up your own questions for each category and don't be afraid to mix it up.

Hopes and Dreams - such as, "what is the happiest life you can imagine?"

The Fun Things - "what upcoming movie release are you most looking forward to?"

About Us - such as, "was there a specific moment when you realized you are in love with me?"

Work Life - "what is the most challenging aspect of your job?"

Emotions - such as, "when were you the most afraid?" Or "what was the best day of your life so far?"

Other Relationships - "who are you closest to in your family?"

By building our relationship skills and communicating effectively while utilizing exercises that enhance the connection between the couple, we can help ensure that we have a strong and long-lasting relationship. While there is no one set exercise that you can engage in to strengthen the relationship or to ward off separation or divorce, utilizing the exercises above can help you find your 'best practice' for your relationship.

Chapter 9: Nonverbal Communication in Your Relationship

Whenever we are having a conversation or otherwise interact with our partner or anyone else, we constantly – unconsciously – give off wordless, or nonverbal clues and signals. From the way we sit, how much eye contact is made, hand or body gestures we make and even how fast and loud we speak can convey some very strong, albeit unintended, messages. Remember that one look your mom could give you as a child that meant you were in deep trouble? She never had to say a word, you could just tell that you were in serious trouble. Almost the whole gamut of emotions can be expressed with a look, smile, sigh, or bob of the head and we have to be careful because the human brain processes both the verbal and nonverbal communication at the same time and can instantly detect when the words don't match the body language.

Many times, what you say with your mouth versus your body language are two completely different things. When we are faced with these sorts of mixed messages then we have to choose which one to give more credence to and invariably we unconsciously the nonverbal message because we feel it conveys their true feelings.

We have to remember that the way we look, react, and even our movements tell our partner how well we're listening and whether we are being truthful or not. When our nonverbal cues lineup with the words that we are saying then we increase trust and build a better rapport but when they don't match up it can create mistrust and tension. All nonverbal communication can easily be misinterpreted and may cause issues within the relationship.

We use our hands when we speak, especially if we are arguing or having a heated discussion. Hand gestures can have different meanings at different times and vary by location so you must always take care to avoid any miscommunication or misinterpretation.

Your face can convey your emotions without you uttering a word and unlike hand gestures, your facial expressions are almost universally identical. Striving to maintain a neutral expression during a conversation, especially if you are in the listening phase, will help avoid derailing the conversation.

Be conscious of your posture and body movements. Remember that folded arms can signal that you are shutting yourself off or are being defensive. On the other hand, sitting forward in your chair can indicate that you are listening raptly.

Maintain eye contact and remember that the way you look at them can convey interest or hostility as well as affection or loathing.

Don't forget to touch. A light hand on the arm or a firm grip of the shoulder communicate almost as much as our spoken words.

Sometimes nonverbal communication can cause others to feel uncomfortable. For example, if someone stands very close to you then you may feel that they are taking up your personal space. If someone's tone of voice sounds sarcastic we may feel that they are making fun of us, even though their words weren't. Most of the time our nonverbal communication is telegraphed unconsciously and shouldn't be seen as intentional. Many times we really don't mean to do it but we can't seem to be able to communicate effectively without it.

Of course, nonverbal communication can also be useful and very reassuring to our partner. Smiling at them while they are trying to apologize, lightly touching their arm during a difficult time or conversation, moving your chair or yourself closer to them, and even a soft tone of voice are all ways that the nonverbal side of things can help increase the closeness between you two.

When we use nonverbal communication to accent a message, it can help enhance the understanding. If you're telling your spouse something and while you're speaking, you see them nodding, that indicates that you are probably both on the same page. If your partner tells you that they are fine with a decision you made but they are frowning or their voice is shaking, you may want to have further discussion on the matter because the nonverbal cues are telling you that something else may be going on.

Nonverbal cues can have several different outcomes, such as accenting or complementing the verbal message, contradict the message you are trying to convey, simply repeat or echo your message, or completely contradict what you have just said.

Chapter 10: Sexual Communication in Your Relationship

Sex can be one of the most difficult topics for couples to have a serious and open conversation about. Because of the inherent intimate nature of sex itself, many feel too ashamed or embarrassed to initiate a discussion on what they like and don't like in the bedroom and they end up either feeling resentful or just settling for what they get. Just as with any aspect of the relationship it is extremely important that couples be able to communicate on a two-way street.

A really good way to start it simply by trying a little debriefing pillow-talk. Be specific but keep your comments positive and use phrases such as, "I really liked when you..." or "maybe next time we could..."

If that doesn't sound appealing try setting a time where there won't be any distractions and have a little one-on-one meeting. This will give you both time to prepare and you can even suggest that you each make a small list of items you'd like to discuss, i.e. turn-ons/turn-offs. If you try this I would suggest that you keep it positive, low key, and that you take turns listing them off one at a time and give each other a chance for clarifying questions. However, remember that the meeting is not to critique or to voice grievances so that no one has a reason to throw up their defense shields.

If talking at all about the subject is unappealing at the time, suggest that you each write a letter. This can give you the opportunity to sort your thoughts and ideas and take away any chance of the conversation devolving into an argument. Make your letters clear and concise and again try to remain completely positive without making any negative comments about your partner or their performance. Remember the "I feel...", "I want...", and "I need..."

You can also get books on the subject or just visit a local bookstore or library together and when you see something that you like, point it out. Make it a game. Order the Kama Sutra and pick three things out that you know that you like are that you would like to try and your partner has to choose one of them to complete. The next time is their turn to select three things.

And of course, there is always porn. Pick something out together, I suggest amateur as opposed to Pro and watch together. When a particular scene or position catches your interest, point it out and say something like "maybe that's something we can try." And if you'd prefer to watch it separately and then discuss, I would suggest either taking notes or again picking out three things that your partner can choose from.

One of the fun solutions is to just try and show them. When you are making love and they do something that you like, tell them right then and there. Don't expect them to read your body language or to just know what you like, take the opportunity to teach them the things that you enjoy. Talking during the act of lovemaking can sometimes enhance the overall pleasure for some people as well. The same goes for if they do something that you don't care for but just remember to make your comments non-negative or judgmental. Stick with the "I" comments.

Now, what about the other awkward conversation that can come up regarding not enough or having too much sex? Everyone has the right at any time to say no to sex and we shouldn't depend on body language to give them the hint that we're not interested. If you don't want to, say no. It doesn't matter what your reasons are or even if you've been with them before. No means no. And of course, we also have the right to change our mind even during sex. Maybe it doesn't feel right are you just not comfortable. You can stop at any time you want and hopefully your relationship is healthy enough that your partner does not make you feel bad or guilty about stopping the act.

Again, these can be a tricky discussion to initiate or to be confronted with. That's why it is important that we remember the points we've already discussed. There are a few additional exercises couples can utilize that may help in this area.

Everybody gets tired, has long weeks or late nights, or just doesn't feel in the mood, but intimacy is an extremely important aspect of every relationship. Start with picking one night a week for a 'date night' that is set in stone and make sure that you follow through with it. Disconnect, shut out the outside world, and spend the evening as just the two of you and let the night take its course. This doesn't mean that you have to have sex on every date night but it will give you more quality time together and ensure that you have a better opportunity for the sparks to get to flying.

Date night also works if things are going the complete opposite direction and the frequency is just too much. At least at this time. Setting 1 - 3 nights a week aside as those special nights with the others for resting or just quality time, together or alone if you need some 'me' time, can be the perfect way to comfortably slow things down.

The biggest thing that you want to keep in mind is that just suffering in silence or settling for what you're getting will leave you feeling dissatisfied, disappointed, or frustrated. While it can sometimes be an embarrassing topic to discuss, utilizing the above pointers and tips are a great way to get the ball rolling without fear of hurting feelings or being ashamed.

Chapter 11: Communication at the Beginning of Budding Relationships

If you take the time to open good lines of communication at the beginning of a relationship it can help you immensely as you move forward together. Of course, it goes without saying that honesty is extremely important at this time so no matter what, be honest with yourself and with your partner. In this chapter, I'm going to cover several key areas and ideas, as well as give you tips for getting some of those awkward conversations started.

Of course, sex is generally a big part of any relationship but it is usually even more so at the beginning. While these can be some of the most difficult conversations to have, especially with a new partner, there are certain ones that you will want to have even before you have sexual relations.

Here are a few of them for you:

What type of relationship are they looking for? Friendly or romantic? Sexual or non-sexual? Committed or non-committed? Monogamous or not? If you don't match up here you may want to reconsider going any further?

When was the last time they were tested for an STD/STI? Which ones were they tested for and what were the results? How many partners have they been with since their last test? Did they use protection? This is also a good time to ask if they have ever shared a needle with someone for tattoos, drugs, or piercings because unfortunately some STI's are transmitted this way.

What about birth control? Which methods do they prefer/use? Is there any possibility of a current pregnancy? Are they open to the possibility of pregnancy? Protecting yourselves from unintended STI's or pregnancies shows that you are responsible and that you care, setting some solid groundwork for open lines of communication. And just remember that the best time to discuss safe sex is before you move to the bedroom. A really good way to start the discussion is by telling them that you truly care about them and you want to ensure that you're both protecting each other and the relationship. You may want to start by voicing your own preferences first as this may make your partner feel more comfortable with the discussion. In this day and age, it is also not a bad idea to go get tested together for mutual support.

The same goes for safer-sex. Do they utilize dental dam or other barriers? What activities do they enjoy without the use of barriers? There are all important conversations to have on this subject and should be discussed as early in the relationship as possible. It is completely natural to feel a little embarrassed bringing the subject up but both you and your partner will be glad you did. Take the guesswork out discuss it early on.

Reflecting back to our previous chapter this is a perfect time to communicate your likes/dislikes when it comes to the bedroom. As you explore and get to know one another sexually, educate them on what kind of touch you enjoy or where and how you like to be kissed. You can and should also take this chance to set any boundaries that you are just not willing to try. Is there anywhere that you don't like being touched or kissed? Tell them now because remember, that shudder can be misinterpreted as joy and pleasure unless you articulate and let them know.

Are there activities or fantasies that you *know* you want to explore? Maybe there are some that you'd like to talk about or even role play or act out. Just remember to be receptive to listening to your partner's desires as well so again it is important to discuss boundaries before having this discussion to avoid making this conversation turn awkward. If you aren't comfortable discussing your fantasies you can try themed porn movies or books and share them together and when the time is right, start the conversation on it with something like, "I enjoyed the ___ scene. Maybe that's something we can try."

Something you both may find useful, and maybe even a little exciting, is making a yes/no/maybe chart. You both go off on your own and list out the things you know you enjoy (Yes), ones you don't like or are not willing to try (No), and then the one you might be interested in. Once complete then share your lists with each other and perhaps flip a coin to see who gets to have one of their Yeses used tonight. This can open some wonderful door for communication and also give you some revealing insight on one another.

Many people learn what they like and don't like by having sex with a partner while others utilize masturbation to get to know their bodies. When you learn how to give yourself orgasms it can make it easier to do so with a partner. Do you like it fast or slow? How much pressure feels good? What makes you uncomfortable? Once you know how to please yourself it is much easier to be able to show your partner how to touch you. You can also crank this up a notch by masturbating in front of each other so you can show them exactly how and then work it into mutual masturbation and take it slow, talk to each other and verbalize clearly when they do something right or wrong.

While talking about sex can be a little awkward or even scary, it can also be very eye-opening and even a turn-on. You can always start the conversation about sex by directly asking them what feels good or what kind of bedroom fun they are interested in. And then you can follow-up by letting them know what feels good to you or what you are wanting to try.

Chapter 12: Communication in the Marriage

Having that two-way street open line of communication is a must-have for any marriage to be successful. Many divorces could be turned around if the spouses simply improved the ways in which they communicate. Simple bad habits are often the ones that get couples into trouble and once the marriage detours onto a rough road, it is very easy for negativity to grow. From there it is easy for the problems to escalate as the couple repeats the same mistakes over and over. However, some of those bad habits and simple communication mistakes can be easily be resolved with just a little effort.

Yelling

Many times, when we are angry we immediately start to raise our voice, sometimes just to release or express the tension of the situation. All too often we end up causing more tension and trouble because we take the easy option of yelling at each other. While releasing this tension by yelling may feel satisfying, it is usually short-lived because what we say in anger can sometimes be hurtful and is likely to escalate the argument.

We release a lot of negative emotions when we yell and from that point forward it can be extremely difficult to communicate. Those emotions will overshadow everything else that you are trying to discuss because the negativity will be what captures your partner's attention the most. And because you have now set them up to be defensive as opposed to being an understanding and responsive, they will likely miss the other points of your conversation or may even misunderstand the entire reason for the discussion in the first place.

Yelling immediately sets the groundwork for a heated exchange of emotions rather than open communication. Emotional exchanges can easily divert into an extremely destructive habit and we have to change so that we are communicating in a way that lets us voice our feelings, frustrations, and emotions so that we can move past them together. For our message to be clear, we have to learn to keep our emotions and check.

If you find that emotions are getting too heated a great way to reduce the stress and distract you from the hot emotions is to take a break from the conversation for a 15-minute workout. It is kind of hard to remain angry or to focus on anything other than yourself when you're trying to catch your breath and all of the good endorphins can actually help calm you down.

And of course, if you detect the conversation detouring into a yelling match you can always use that pause button. Take 15 to 30 minutes away from each other and go do something you enjoy such as watching TV, or reading a magazine or book or even taking a shower or bath. This will give you both time to calm down and to think about how you want to approach the discussion. You'll find that you can get through problems together a lot more easily if you are on each other side instead of pushing each other away.

Name Calling

In the same way that our voice can rise with our temper, our vocabulary can devolve very rapidly. While pet names can be cute and endearing, words do hurt and may cause irreparable damage if we resort to name-calling during an argument. While it may seem appropriate at the time and movies and TV shows like to focus and poke fun at name-calling during arguments, hitting someone with a dirty or inappropriate name during the heat of an argument can have more sting than a physical strike. It can be exceedingly difficult to forgive someone when they stoop to this level and sometimes the hurt can last for days or even longer. Unfortunately, sometimes resulting in the breakup of the relationship.

Once you tear into that can of worms it leaves you open for a return volley and you just might not like what you hear back. This can end up diluting the issue and lead you both into a shouting match filled with hurtful names that neither of you will be able to take back. Again, this is why it is important to take a step back or to use that pause button when we detect that tempers are flaring. Don't say something that you're going to regret. Think before you speak.

When It's ALL about "I" And Not "Us."

While it is important that we began many conversations utilizing the "I" starters, we have to remember that the central focus of a marriage must come back to "us." Take a look at your regular day-to-day conversations that you have with your spouse and see if you see behaviors that may need to change. Do they seem to revolve around your mood, day, plans, or what you expect from your spouse? If so then you may want to start peppering your conversations with questions about your partner's plans/mood/etc. to help even out your daily interactions.

Do small little things throughout the day that let your partner know you're thinking about them. Whether with a flirty text or a quick call just to say hello, when you communicate for no other reason than to communicate our love or affection it helps solidify the building blocks for that two-way street of communication.

Try to be more thoughtful, considerate, and generous toward your spouse and they are likely to reciprocate. Try to surprise them by knocking out one of their chores for them or by planning a special meal that you know they truly enjoy. If you focus on improving in these areas and keep it consistent, your spouse will eventually say or do something in kind. These kinds of behaviors can really help strengthen the foundation and nurture a great marriage.

Of course, old habits are hard to break and it will take some practice to break some of these common communication mistakes but it can be amazing how just a few small changes can change the energy of a marriage. If at first, you don't see your spouse reciprocating, don't give up. At first, it is easy to want to give up if they haven't seemed to notice but if you keep going you'll find that the more you act with generosity, the more loving and generous you feel toward your spouse.

Competitive Attitudes in Marriage

Everybody likes to win and many of us are competitive by nature but while we may strive to be the top dog or to stay ahead in many areas of our lives, our marriages should not be one of. If one of you is always the winner, both of you lose. If you try to win every argument every time you may end up hurting or even demoralizing your partner more so than anything else.

Stop and think about why you feel the need to always win. Sometimes emotional insecurities can cause us to overcompensate by trying to look superior to our spouses. If we stay on top it is easier to feel stronger and more confident but having the weight of us constantly over them can actually make them feel insecure. Remember, communicating is not about being right or winning but about working as a team. If you find yourself mentally making bullet points for every disagreement for you to make your point or to win the argument you could end up doing a lot more harm than good.

Never Wrong

Whether you admit it or not, you are not perfect and you will make mistakes. While it can sometimes be hard to admit when we're wrong if we want to have a strong relationship there are going to be times when we have to apologize or admit that we were wrong. Don't be afraid of showing weakness by admitting you're wrong. That kind of stuff is for teenagers. If you try to "always be right" or try to deny or rationalize your behavior then your relationship will turn unhealthy fast. "I'm sorry" and "I was wrong" are all too underused in relationships but can go a long way toward building a better relationship.

Chapter 13: Communication Through Hardships

Unfortunately, life tends to throw many hurdles, obstacles, and curveballs in our way, and in any relationship, it can be difficult to communicate effectively during these hard times. Whether it's a new baby, new job, relocation, or financial difficulties the reality is that all couples eventually face tough times. It usually is very painful to be in a situation where you have no control and unfortunately some people just aren't able to get back up on their own when life knocks them off their feet and they need a little help.

This is especially true when it comes to relationships. If one person is feeling overwhelmed by the trials and tribulations and they do not feel supported can communicate, it can deteriorate the marriage quickly. This is why building strong two-way communication is so vital early on in the relationship, you have to be able to discuss the sometimes embarrassing hardships and face them together.

In a healthy relationship, we can never deny, minimize, or disregard the problem at hand when we are faced with a challenging situation. We must acknowledge situations and work together toward a resolution. Your active listening skills and just being there for your spouse when they need you are two of the biggest things you can utilize to help see you through the hard times.

One place that may sound strange to start is by sitting down together and discussing other bad times you have both experienced, whether together or separately. The reason for this is to show yourself and each other that you've faced tough times in the past and were able to get through them. Most of us are usually convinced that this current hardship is the worst experience of our life but when we stop to think about all the times we were able to get through other life-changing events it can actually make us feel stronger and more confident facing this one together.

Stressful situations can be overwhelming, but if we let the conversation become overheated, it can be nearly impossible for either of you to make a rational decision. While it is true that running away from your problems never helps, that doesn't mean that you can't hit that pause button that we've discussed too much. This is where it becomes really important to remove yourselves from the situation, and the conversation, long enough to give you both time to think clearly and more rationally. However, it doesn't mean that you have to ingrain yourselves so deeply into the issue that you end up with blinders on to the other aspects of your life.

If you find that you just can't seem to have a discussion on the topic without it turning heated, then it may be useful to fall back on some of the other techniques we've discussed. One of the better ones that I have found for these difficult situations is to utilize letter writing. Don't use text. Text can feel too impersonal and it will seem more from the heart if it is a handwritten letter. Remember to keep emotion out of it, make it concise, and ensure that you list every key area needing to be discussed and any ideas that you have for resolving the current hardship. After this initial discussion, you may want to take a break to give your partner the opportunity to respond back with their own letter to forgo any defensiveness.

In any relationship, there can come a time when we have to make the choice to forgive. No matter what the reason is for our resentment or anger we are going to have to let it go if the relationship has any hope of survival. We have to make the decision to accept what happened and no longer hold it against our partner. This will let you move forward because you are no longer focusing on the negative feelings and thoughts.

As we discussed, relationships are built on trust and without it, they will die, dry up, and blow away. We can easily start to build trust when we are reliable and follow through on even the little things in our daily lives. This makes the hardships so much easier to deal with because your partner will feel safe and secure knowing that you will do what needs to be done and what you say you'll do. Consistently keeping your promises is one sure way to build your partner's trust.

The same goes if you find yourself trying to regain trust. Breaking someone's trust can be a very difficult hardship to overcome and unfortunately, many relationships do not survive it. Following through and keeping your promises on little things can show your spouse that you are serious and can be trusted to keep your word. While I never recommend being untruthful or untrustworthy in any relationship, as we all know it, unfortunately, happens all too often. No matter the reason for the break in trust it can be almost an impossible pill to swallow and it will take time, energy, and work to rebuild it back to the levels you desire.

Relationships are priceless but require a lot of work and energy. Many spouses neglect to put energy into their relationship and expect it to work out on its own and they forget to make their spouse feel special, appreciated, and sometimes even loved. If you want to keep the relationship thriving you must actively pursue each other throughout the relationship. This includes both through the good times and the bad. Putting energy into the relationship can be even more important during the hardships and simply holding hands, looking into each other's eyes while you speak, or just setting aside time for just the two of you can communicate to your partner that you truly do care. The current issue at hand may affect the other aspects of your lives but it doesn't have to have a negative effect on the relationship. Actively pursuing your partner through the hardships helps affirm that you are on the same team and that together you can conquer anything.

Patience is a virtue that will come in quite handy throughout the relationship but even more so as you face hardships together. Don't let the hardship damage your relationship. Stay away from sarcasm, lecturing, swearing, and name-calling and realize that if you are not careful the hardship can indeed adversely affect you and your loved one's relationship. You will find that things work out so much better when you turn toward your partner instead of away from them.

Work together and shift gears in your mindset. Stop thinking "poor us" or focusing solely on one fix to the issue. Actively pursue other strategies and ask for your partner's input. What are some other ways to resolve the current hardship? How can you learn from this situation? How can you use it to grow closer together?

Breaking up your routine can be fun at any time in a relationship, but it can be extremely helpful during those tough times. Get out together and try something new even if it's just taking a drive, going for a stroll, or trying a new restaurant it can help alleviate the negative pressure on you and bring you closer together by helping keep those lines of communication open.

Never try to assign blame even when blame is warranted. Pointing fingers will never help the situation and we have to remember that everyone makes mistakes. For a healthy relationship we have to forgive but of course, this doesn't mean that you're condoning the behavior or actions of the current situation. You are just working together to move past it.

It may be easier for you to view hardships like climbing a huge mountain and use these five steps to help get you through:

Bring supplies - find activities that energize you and your partner. It will take quite a bit of an effort to get over this mountain.

Create a map - consider each of your concerns, what you would like to accomplish, and how you think you should get there.

Bring a compass - this is simply setting benchmarks to let you see your progress up the mountain.

Break up the duties - create a plan that lays out exactly what each of you will do to resolve the situation. It may be helpful to set a specific timetable for each of the duties to be completed and in what order they should be attacked. This doesn't mean that you cannot work together, it's just to help lighten the workload for you both. This is also a good place to schedule some time for you two to be alone. Think of it as a base camp. Don't get hung up on the issue and set some time aside for some quality time.

Get an aerial view - set aside specific time to discuss the situation, your concerns, and how it is affecting you. Listen to each other and thoroughly take into consideration any ideas that are brought forth. Comfort each other. Take the time to keep each other warm and to keep the other from falling off the ledge. It is usually only going to be you two at the summit and you need to work together to keep each other safe and happy.

Whether or not the outcome of your choices proved to be effective or not, there always comes the time that we have to accept them and move forward. Be sure to take a moment to thank each other for the parts played getting through the hardship together. Don't think about who did what or who didn't do something, focus on the positives and move forward.

To move forward together we must have those open lines of communication. Don't dwell on the past or coulda/woulda/shoulda's and move forward together using it as a learning experience and strengthening your relationship together. Strong relationships take a lot of work and don't just happen overnight and having that two-way street of communication can help you make your relationship strong and long-lasting.

Conclusion

I want to congratulate you for making it through to the end of *Communication for Couples*.

As you have learned, clear and effective communication is an essential piece of the foundation that all relationships need to thrive and survive. In a world where many opt to talk to their loved ones using some sort of device, isn't the time *now* to get back to the basics of communication and polish up our skills to ensure that our relationships are not left to rot at their core.

I hope that you have discovered some methods that you think will work wonders for you and your partner. Everyone could use a little tweaking when it comes to redefining the communication barriers in relationships. No couple deserves to have to climb over the tall walls we build around ourselves. Communication is the one thing that can break down impassable walls and bring two people closer together.

I challenge you to take at least one thing away from what you have read and start applying it *today* to begin the process of bettering your relationship. The best part is, you could use many of the techniques found in this book to better communication within your non-romantic relationships in life as well!

So, what are you waiting for? The only thing standing between you and a better relationship is finding the motivation to take action and start using the strategies you have acquired!

Did you find this book to be valuable and of use to you in any way? If so, please take a moment to leave me a review on Amazon. It is always appreciated! I wish you the best of luck in rediscovering why you fell in love with your partner through the avenues of effective communication.

Made in the USA
San Bernardino, CA
23 December 2018